NOTICE ME!

for Jerry
+
Dru——→

Look up↑

Brothers + Sisters

with Love

Ric Masters
12/5/86

For Parents,
Students,
Faculty
& Friends

# NOTICE ME!

*A selection of poems
and song lyrics*

*by RIC MASTEN*

SUNFLOWER INK
Palo Colorado Canyon
Carmel, Calif. 93923

# ACKNOWLEDGEMENTS

Most of the poems and song lyrics in this collection were selected from the books THE VOICE OF THE HIVE, DRAGONFLIES, CODFISH & FROGS, STARK NAKED, EVEN AS WE SPEAK and THEY ARE ALL GONE NOW, published by Sunflower Ink.

Cover artwork by Caroll McKanna Halley.

*NOTICE ME! Parents, Students, Faculty & Friends* produced by Clack & Nichols, A Partnership, 522 North Grant, Odessa, Texas 79761. Telephone number (915) 337-8511.

(paperback) 9 8 7 6 5 4 3 2 1

Library of Congress Catalogue Card No. 85-082615
ISBN 0-931104-17-3

for *Sharon Christa McAuliffe*
*(page 77)*

# CONTENTS

INTRODUCTION

*NOTICE ME!* is Ric Masten's response to years of requests from parents and teachers who have watched him weave his spell over children of all ages, and have asked themselves, "How can we keep this level of enthusiasm and openness alive after this man leaves us?"

Just watch the small and reluctant show of raised hands as Ric opens his performance with the question, "How many of you kids like poetry?" Then see the enthusiasm awaken, as with songs and poems and funny and poignant anecdotes, these young "non-poets" are won over to a different perception. "A poem is the lyric to a song, and don't you all like songs?" A resounding "YES!" the children shout out. And then Ric will sing a rousing rendition of the first poem-song that made him money (16,000 dollars of it, kids!), "I Was a Teenage Creature," as an example of an "F-" poem *not* written from the heart. And then while the audience is still laughing over the deeds of the hairy teenager, Ric will zoom in with lessons on how to write an "A+" poem, one that *does* come from the heart. He tells how to "corral" feelings—how to construct a poem like one might build a corral for an illusive horse, with ideas as the posts, technique as the railings, and the horse within as the deep feeling that needs to be captured and expressed.

Here is a grown man in front of a crowd of young strangers, not hesitating to share his most intimate thoughts and feelings, his joys and sorrows and laughter. Trepidation about the mysteries of poetry seep away, and Ric Masten is spinning his magic again.

Since 1968, Ric has left his Big Sur home overlooking the Pacific Ocean and has struck out in his van on annual cross-country treks. For five years, Ric toured as the Billings Lecturer, under the auspices of the Unitarian Universalist Association (other Billings lecturers have been Margaret

Mead and Carl Rogers). Then as his reputation grew, Ric traveled independently, and is now accompanied by his wife Billie Barbara, a poet and performer in her own right. Their itinerary is determined by a heavy schedule of college and university engagements. Along the way, however, Ric will sing and recite wherever he is invited or needed—in prisons, churches, nursing homes, at AA groups, on radio and TV talk shows, and perhaps most importantly of all, in elementary, middle, and high schools. "Most importantly," because in an age dominated by television, computers, and impersonal methods of communication, Ric Masten offers our children a real way out of what often seems to be a desperately lonely and unfeeling world.

Using his own life as a candid example laid bare, Ric shows young people how to look honestly and clearly at their feelings, and how to express them in a verbal or poetic form. True communication is a measure of freedom, and communication is the rare gift that Ric has to share with and teach to our children.

Readers may use this book as a teaching guide, or as a reminder of how Ric Masten's poetry and songs have moved their students and children, or (for those who have not met or heard the author) as an invitation to explore a unique way of coming to terms with the vagaries of life that face us all, young and old alike.

*NOTICE ME!* is divided into four sections: "Parents," "Students," "Faculty," and "Friends." It is prefaced by the title poem, which addresses an all-important and often-ignored fact—our children need to be *recognized* by US, their parents, teachers, and friends.

In "Parents," Ric's poems show how he himself has dealt with the coming-of-age of his own children. We see the love, the worries, the humor (read "A Tar Baby") involved. "Students" gathers together the song lyrics that Ric has used so successfully in his school performances, starting with the kindergarteners' "Evy Ivy Over" and culminating with two poignant lyrics for teenagers, "Who's Wavin'" and "Loneliness."

"Faculty" addresses the need for empathy with children, and the problems facing a teacher with the seemingly impossible task of assigning a grade to a student's dream (or poem), and who may have to deal with his or her own professional burn-out. "Friends" is composed of a sampling of letters from academicians who have experienced and been touched by Ric's poetry.

Most of these poems were written a number of years ago, when Ric's own four children were growing up. Ric is now grappling with another stage of his life—which he laughingly claims only gives birth to poems about "death, divorce, suicide and despair." We are indeed fortunate that he has taken the time to go back over this important material, and arrange it in such a useful, coherent, and evocative format.

Ric Masten has called himself a "cheerleader for poetry." Certainly he strips the poetic form of its strangeness and unobtainability, and shows us how we might express the humor, compassion, sadness, and love of our own lives. . . and perhaps with his encouragement even "corral" a poem of our own.

Embree De Persiis
Big Sur, California
March 1986

put me in your human eye
come taste the bitter tears that i cry
touch me with your human hand
hear me with your ear
and notice me!
damn you — notice me!
                    i'm here

we can't be bothered now
the distant voices said
when i came to share
the butterfly i found
and i'd look up into the nostrils
of the faces overhead
but i never caught the giants
lookin' down

# NOTICE ME!

yeah, i'm the poor misshapen figure
in the backroom of your home
your little baby's gone
and blown his mind
he's at the nursery window
standin' all alone
trying to catch the eye
of the blind

put me in your human eye
come taste the bitter tears that i cry
touch me with your human hand
hear me with your ear
but notice me
damn you — notice me!
                    i am

# I.
# PARENTS

# THE COFFEE TABLE DANCER

i remember parties
when i was only five
standing at the window
watching the guests arrive
they'd step into the hallway
laughing too loud i'd think
keeping their fingers busy
with a cigarette and a drink
and i'd be in the corner
in a white shirt and short pants
standing in the corner
just waiting for my chance
   the coffee table dancer
   oh just you wait and see

they'd sit down together
to play at their head games
to quote the books they were reading
and drop the authors' names
the talk was always liberal
around the onion dip
but lonely were the faces
with the talking lips
and i'd be in the corner
and not receive a glance
standing in the corner
just waiting for my chance
   the coffee table dancer
   oh just you wait and see

they'd interrupt each other
fighting for the floor
to mourn the League of Nations
and weep about the war
and when their lips were finished
with what was in their head
they'd fall strangely silent

3

for it had all been said
and then i'd leave the corner
for this would be my chance
to jump up on the table
and do my little dance
   the coffee table dancer
    see me — see me — see me

and now here i am before you
and i think i'm living a lie
what devious means i'm using
just to catch your eye
and was i not more honest
when i was young and green
coffee table dancing
just so i'd be seen?
hey — you there in the corner
won't you take this chance
to jump up on the table
and join me in a dance
   coffee table dancers
   aren't we all
   aren't we all
   aren't we all?

# ELLEN

my youngest daughter
likes to ride
to the mailbox with me

she fetches the mail
while i turn the car around
then she climbs into the back seat

and doles out my letters
slowly
inspecting each envelope

till i am infuriated
and turn red
and shout at her

Ellen!
gimme
the letters!

my youngest daughter likes to do this
it is one of the few times
she has my full attention

# CHILD PRODIGY

when he was one year old
he was already considered
a world class player
at tic-tac-toe

in his second season
he became a noted semanticist
pointing out to his elders that "maybe"
was just a slow "no"

he was deeply into Moby Dick
at three
beginning every conversation with
"call me Ishmael!"

at four
a recognized poet himself
"till i discovered they were crickets
i had thought they were the stars"

but i knew he was more than bright
when going against popular opinion
he forgave his father for all those
painful trips out to the woodshed

"i had to be whipped"
he said
"you can't send a kid to his room
when the kid has a circus in his head"

# THE PUNCH & JUDY SHOW

trying hard to understand human nature
i
having pacifist leanings
find my son learning karate
breaking bricks with his bare hands
so that he could kill a man
in two seconds
he says smiling
as i go up the wall
and i
being the son of militant ex-catholic
atheist parents
get myself ordained a minister
much to the disgrace of my old mother
whose reedy voice calls me on the phone

    ricky! — she squeaks

as always speaking
like a Punch and Judy show
and i as always looking
for the alligator to jump up
and hit her with a stick

    ricky! — she squawks

    you're not gonna let them
    put Reverend in front of your name
    in the phone book are you?

now
i suppose all this explains
why the grandparents and the grandchildren
usually get along so well

they have a common enemy

# RELATIVITY

have you noticed
that everyone else's kid
seems able
to understand Einstein's
theory of relativity?

while yours
can't seem to find the door

we laugh now

but yesterday
a father's misgivings
were kept locked away
on the third floor
like
idiot children

# SPITTING IMAGE

there have been two creatures
on this earth
i could never get the best of
my dog
and my mother

whenever i would catch
either one of them
up to no good
    chewing a shoe
    sneaking through a drawer
one would become deathly ill
the other
pee on the floor

the dog is gone now
piddling around out there
beyond my kick and frustrated shout
and feeling a sudden chill today
i pulled on a sweater
and at the sleeve
guess whose hand came out
    shaking the thermometer

# A TAR BABY

she waits in the brier patch
     sweet as honey
     tacky as tar
in her thorny ambushes she waits
and practices her guitar and her
     i don't know
     what you're talking about
song and dance
     till i come along
     her half-witted son
she'd say
     and i would agree
for anyone with a lick of sense
knows enough to leave a tar baby be

still
through much perseverance
       i've learned
ways
to handle the whole messy business
of a child-parent relationship
     and can do it these days
     with a certain dispatch
      and expertise

the safest approach of course
     is to stay out of reach
and when least expected sneak up
     on the snare and yell
     tar baby
     i love you
then run like hell
sometimes i can be two blocks away
before she knew i was there

or if you're a glutton for punishment
you can survive keeping in mind

the fact that you deal
with something as primal as
            the La Brea Tar Pit
        a quagmire of glutinous stuff
            that sucked in
            and gummed up
the fearsome tyrannosaurus
but these being civilized times
        if it seems important enough
        go ahead pay the tar baby a call
            do it
put yourself through it
maybe twice a year
            but that's all
however
never stand outside that door
thinking you know what it's all about
thinking
        this time i'm going in there
and i'm gonna straighten
            the tar baby out
oh yes
let me say this in closing
my oldest daughter
has turned twenty-two
and someone is coming
            Br'er Rabbit
            is that you?

# PISTACHIO NUTS

i'm embarrassed to think
that i was eleven years old
before some skinny kid
brought Santa Claus down in flames
right in the middle of the noon recess
how i remained
among the faithful all those years
i'll never know
the playing fields of grammar school
are swarming with doubting Thomases
shooting marbles for keeps
anyway
i went home mad as hell
demanding the truth from my mother

i think you're old enough to handle it
she said
and then in one fell swoop
wiped out not only Santa
but the Easter Bunny as well

however twenty-nine years later
i'm really kind of glad
some bearded dirty old man
doesn't slide down my chimney
every twenty-fifth of December
and eat up forty-nine cents
worth of pistachio nuts

like the evening i'm driving home
after putting in
eight hours on a cement crew
feeling tired and dry and dusty
and sorry for myself
so i stop for a treat
a cold can of beer
to hold between my knees

on the road home
and the aforementioned forty-nine cents
worth of pistachio nuts

well i guess i've been so worried
about the conservative faces
in the pontiacs and cadillacs
with stars and stripes stuck to everything
that i just naturally give a lift
to every long-haired freaky kid i see
and these two were beautiful
in their costumes
on their way to Big Sur
my kind of people
peace brother
peace brother
i was twice blessed
Friar Tuck and Robin are alive and well
on the highways of America

have a pistachio nut
said the Sheriff of Nottingham
and the cellophane bag
did make a happy crinkling sound
as it emptied
in my brother's hands

they are right you know
i am not to be trusted
i do grow tired of carrying you twelve miles
and paying forty-nine cents
worth of pistachio nuts for this privilege
so
this is as far as i go
i think you're old enough to handle it

there ain't no Santa Claus!

13

# MISSING PERSON REPORT

i distinctly heard you say
you'd be home by ten
and here it is way past one

    late again — the traffic no doubt
    a breakdown — no — a blowout — flares
    in the night — at the hairpin turn
    and the hee-haw hee-haw
    of an ambulance running the lights

    me
    in a ratty old bathrobe
    receiving the call from the highway patrol
    unshaven — disheveled — at the morgue
    grieving out loud as they pull the drawer
    and lift the shroud

    me
    putting aside the hurt
    putting aside the pain
    putting together
    a meaningful memorial service
    down to the last detail
    to the brave smile — the gray rain
    the dirt pile nicely covered by astro turf

    me
    choosing the priest
    the prayer
    the closing song and then

you
come waltzing along
as if nothing had happened
as if nothing were wrong

in the unexpected absence of a loved one
why is a head-on collision easier to imagine

than the thought of them out there
winning the irish sweepstakes?

instead of six feet under the sod
why can't we picture them off somewhere
having the time of their lives
with a rich philanthropist
a theatrical agent
or God?

# THE WEANING

after considerable work in the field
i have come to the conclusion
that when it comes to me
and my children
it is easy to say "no" all the time
and it is easy to say "yes" all the time
but it is impossible
to be a logical consistent parent

however
i do not lie awake nights
over this any longer
for to treat children
in a logical consistent fashion
and then turn them out into the world
as we know it
would be a cruel crippling
and inhuman thing to do

it is only fair though
that when the kids have broken loose
and are out on their own
they should receive a hand-written letter
from me their father
expressing my love
and stating that all is forgiven
if they promise not to come home

# DEAR SANTA
*(Country-Western Song Lyric, 1958)*

the wife and i separated
why?...well let's just say because —
and today i got the letter
my boy wrote to Santa Claus
it read...

> dear Santa, bring home my daddy
> on this Christmas day
> mommy has never quit crying
> since daddy went away

> this Christmas forget the presents
> i don't want any toys
> Santa, i just want a daddy
> like other girls and boys

> i guess you know i've been naughty
> don't know why i can't be good
> but Santa if you'll bring my daddy
> i promise i'll act like i should

> dear Santa on Christmas morning
> when i run to see the tree
> there with his arm around mommy
> please have daddy waiting for me

i cried as i read that letter
and i knew that i had done wrong
so i'm going home this Christmas
'cause home is where i belong

Santa, now don't you worry
i'll be beside that tree
and i'll have my arm around mommy
when my boy comes looking for me

# COMING HOME

the continuing story of a traveling salesman
continues
>      this time
>      we find him running
>      out of an airport
>      giftshop
>      with a cap pistol
>      and a doll
>      a surprise for the kids
>      but like oxfords
>      hastily bought
> > > a size too small
(the kids i remembered
were not kids at all)

"i think i've been gone longer than i thought"
>      cried
>      old Saint Nick
>      as ever ho-ho-hoing
>      as ever coming and going
>      giving the children puppies for Christmas
>      never there when the dog died

but it's okay dad
it's all right
they say
>      there is no such thing
>      as a bad parent
they say
>      even people who batter their offspring
>      are doing the best
>      they know how to do

and you can tell that
to the boxes that were never opened
you can tell that to the shoes that pinch

# I, THE CATERPILLAR

i the caterpillar
did see saint butterfly
i was working at my weaving
and i saw her flutter by
and i wondered that a thing
could be so fragile and so frail
dancing on the lilacs
all the way to jail

and i hung her
in a pale white cage
up in a broken tree
and i longed to climb inside her eyes
and listen to the sea
and i would give my body to be lifted
by her wings
but i the caterpillar
am tangled in my strings

for who
would have the grocer
check the items from the list
and when my loves are sleeping
there are eyelids to be kissed
and the yellow bus keeps coming
at four o'clock each day
and i the caterpillar
cannot get away

and if i had a pair of wings
and knew i wouldn't fall
then the simple act of flying
doesn't mean much at all
and if i jumped without them
well i wonder what we'd find
in all the empty rooms

i would go and leave behind

so i the caterpillar
will keep working at my trade
and i won't know what i'm weaving
until i get it made
if i don't believe in butterflies
i can tell you this
we all will do what we must do
simply to exist

                    i, the caterpillar
                    and saint butterfly

# A MEMO FROM THE PAST

at 25
you can't imagine how frustrating it is
to be over 50
trying to explain something
to someone 25

to someone — who is twice as far away
                from tomorrow
                as i am

to someone — on whose person
                things have not begun growing
                and/or
                started dropping off
                and falling out of

to someone — who hasn't yet discovered
                that being old
                feels exactly like being young
                with something wrong

and so
for those of you who maintain
chronological age is irrelevant
i have prepared a statement
to be opened and read when
they themselves turn fifty
a memo that goes:

                greetings
                know-it-all
                and don't say i didn't tell ya so.

(the anticipation of an event such as this
is incentive enough to keep me alive
for another 25 years)

# THE DESERTED ROOSTER

if this were a documentary
Lorne Green would narrate
describing in his big male-animal-world way
the migration
as one by one the fledglings flew the coop
followed by the hen
liberated and running off to join the sisters
cloistered in the halls
of a community college
singing
        Gloria
        Gloria
        Steinem—till it becomes catholic

so far nothing new
children leaving home
a woman's victory
over the empty-nest syndrome
themes done to death

but the deserted rooster is a subject
that has not yet been addressed
we know him
only as that laughable old strutter
preening and parading up and down
involved in his sexual prowess
and the sound of his own voice
up
at an ungodly hour to start the day
it was all part of the job
and there wasn't a problem
when there wasn't a choice

but picture him now
after the exodus
all alone

scratching around in his abandoned domain
looking for a good reason to get up tomorrow
and crow

if this were a documentary
it would end
focused on a stereotype weather vane
rusted on the turning point

in a changing wind

# PARENTS

unopened as yet
the envelope turns in my hand
and
i suppose the Flying Wallendas can
but i never could stand at ease
watching my children
      play in the woods
      play in the trees
so certain was i that they would fall
and they did
and they didn't

but now that they have grown old
as i was then
out on their own
sending messages home
      as to where they are
      and how they've been
the envelope turns in my hand
and nothing has changed at all

# II.
# STUDENTS

# EVY IVY OVER
*(Pre-school.)*

Evy, ivy,
Evy ivy over.
Evy in, ivy out
Evy ivy over.

I woke up this morning
Right at the crack of dawn.
Outside in the street
Strange things were going on.

*Chorus*

Thought we'd been invaded
By men from outer space.
Sounded like the end
Of the human race.

*Chorus*

I could hear an army
Of little tramping feet.
With this battle cry
They came up the street.

*Chorus*

Stopped in front of my house.
It all seemed like a dream.
Would these creatures be
Purple, pink or green?

*Chorus*

Went to meet their leader.
Did I feel like a dope.
There were no men from Mars,
My kids were jumping rope.

# CHICKEN LITTLE
*(Kindergarten–3rd grade.)*


There was a little chicken,
Chicken Little that's him.
Peckin' and a scratchin'
By an oak tree limb.
An acorn fell on Chicken Little's head,
And this is what the little chicken said:

> The sky's fallin'!
> Said Chicken Little.
> The sky's fallin'!
> Said Chicken Little
> That's what Chicken Little said.

He was a little chicken
So he'd started to cry.
Told how he'd been clobbered
By a hunk of sky.
And everyone went runnin' all around
When they were told: The sky's comin' down.

> The sky's fallin'!
> Said Chicken Little.
> The sky's fallin'!
> Said Chicken Little.
> That's what Chicken Little said.

A weepin' and a wailin'
Everybody they hid.
Waitin' for the good Lord
To drop the lid.
But that big sky stayed up where it belonged,
And it was clear the chicken had been wrong.

> It ain't fallin',
> Chicken Little.
> It ain't fallin',
> Chicken Little.
> That's what everybody said.

Now we're all a little chicken
Full of worry and doubt.
But when you get a problem
Just work it out!
And don't you swallow everything you've heard
Or you'll be like that silly little bird.

Chicken Little,
Like Chicken Little.
Chicken Little,
Like Chicken Little.
Don't be a silly little bird.

# HOMESICK SNAIL
*(Kindergarten–3rd grade.)*


Did you ever hear the story
Of the homesick snail?
You'll find him in the garden
At the end of a tearstained trail.
The ant is in his anthill
The bug beneath the stone
But the snail slips down
That winding road
Tryin' to find his home.

> Homesick
> Slidin' along
> Feelin' homesick
> But where
> Does a homesick snail belong?

The spider is contented
In her spider web.
The butterfly right at home
Flyin' overhead
And deep within the woodwork
The termite drills a hall
And each and every cricket
Has his hole in the wall.

> *Chorus*

The fuzzy caterpillar
Is asleep in his cocoon
The angleworm digs underground
Where there's lots of room.
The centipede and beetle
Each have found a place
But the homesick snail
Goes racing round at a snail's pace.

> *Chorus*

I guess he's born to wander
Yes I guess that's all he knows
Cause everytime the snail arrives
He thinks it's time to go.
Sliding down that highway
Down his silver track
Searching for the very thing
He carries on his back.

*Chorus*

We all live in the garden
And I am the snail.

# BOBBLY BUMPER BOOPER
*(Kindergarten–3rd grade.)*


Last night
Bobbly Bumper Booper
And I made a playhouse,
And we shingled our playhouse
With sticks of Juicy Fruit Gum.
Got 'em straight out of the package,
Wrapped in tinfoil,
Sugar powdered
Sticks of Juicy Fruit Gum.

And then it rained.
I dreamed that it rained,
And when the morning came. . . .

Bobbly Bumper Booper
Our playhouse was ruined
Looked like someone had been chewin'
The flavor right out of the gum.
And Bobbly Bumper Booper
Here comes the moral,
With which I'll never quarrel
Don't chew Juicy Fruit Gum
In school!

# THE DIRTY WORD SONG
*(Kindergarten–3rd grade.)*

It's only fair to warn ya 'bout the next song you hear,
It gets a little nasty and it could offend your ear.
You're gonna find the language a trifle strong
'Cause I'm about to sing ya my dirty word song.
    Dirty words, dirty words, I'm gonna say a few
    Real dirty words like . . . . . . . . . doggy poo!

Ya give a boy a pencil and put him in the hall,
Turn your back and dirty words appear on every wall.
But force him to talk naughty for an hour each day
And you'll take all the fun of the dirty words away
    Dirty words, dirty words, boys talk naughty
    They say dirty words like . . . . . . . . . potty!

When your second grader starts sayin' dirty stuff,
Swearin' like a trooper, well it's time to call her bluff.
She likes to think she's bein' real obscene
And she don't even know what the dirty words mean.
    Dirty words, dirty words, she swears like a trooper
    Saying real dirty words like . . . . . . . . . pooper!

Wouldn't it be awful if people didn't swear,
And when ya bang your finger ya jes' give a silent prayer.
If suddenly the dirty words all were clean
Would the poetry improve in the men's latrine?
    Dirty words, dirty words, be glad we got 'em
    Real dirty words like . . . . . . . . . bottom!

I wonder what would happen if no one were profane,
If no one could remember a single dirty name.
I wonder if they'd scribble on the bathroom door
Filthy dirty things like hate and war
    Dirty words, dirty words, there's no excuse for
    Filthy dirty things like hate and war.

# BARBIE DOLL
*(Grades 4, 5 and 6.)*

A slender little waist.
A pretty little face.
That's Barbie with every hair in place
There's no rebellion in a Barbie Doll
There's just a little empty space.

Barbie Doll, Barbie Doll.
Oh, what a perfect world
This world would be
If every little girl were a Barbie!

She loves to look her best
In a new expensive dress.
For Barbie this is happiness.
Invest your money in a Barbie Doll,
She's not the kind to protest.

*Chorus*

When she sees something new
Made of taffeta and blue
Your Barbie has got to have one too
And all the bankers must love Barbie Doll
'Cause they're glad to loan the money to you.

*Chorus*

She sees a lot of Ken
Ah, but he is just a friend.
And Barbie she'll not give in to him.
You've got no problems with your Barbie Doll,
'Cause you can't tell her from him.

*Chorus*

There's not a bit of strife
With a Barbie in your life
With a Barbie for a daughter or a wife.
No, there's not one problem in a Barbie Doll,
And also not a bit of life.

34

# MR. GLUM AND CAPTAIN HAPPY
*(Grades 4, 5 and 6.)*

Mister Glum.
Mister Glum.
He walks the street.
He rides the bus.
Looks the same as all of us.
I know you've seen him going to and from.
And you would never guess that this
Mild-mannered pessimist
Could secretly and suddenly become
Captain Happy!

And what does the Captain say?
    He says:
    Have a good day, have a good day
    Have a good day
    The Captain Happy way.

Mister Glum.
Mister Glum.
Like the super heroes
Of our youth
He ducks into a telephone booth
The magic words are all he has to say.
Then bounding out for all to see
His fingers held up in a V
It's Captain Happy —
Up up and away!

    *Chorus*

Mister Glum.
Mister Glum.
He drops a dime.
He spins the dial
Smiles a silly little smile
Then there's a flash that almost makes you blind
And stepping from a cloud of smoke
He tells a super funny joke

And signals that—
It's Captain Happy time.

*Chorus*

Mister Glum.
Mister Glum.
Oh yes my friends
It's really true
And you'll be super happy too.
The magic words are all you have to say.
So go and find the nearest phone
And call someone you've never known
And spread some joy—
The Captain Happy way!

# WAR PARTY
*(Grades 4, 5 and 6.)*

A wagon train had circled up
This side of Turkey Creek.
Young Tom was in his blanket roll,
His eyes still full of sleep
When the crack of a Sharps 50
Rang in the dawn so cool.
The scout had shot a Pawnee brave
Caught tryin' to steal a mule.
The wagon master passed the word,
That the Pawnee would return.
He said they'd come to take revenge
To plunder and to burn.
It was too late for runnin',
They'd never get away.
And while the camp prepared to fight
Young Tom slipped off to play.

War party's comin'!
War party's comin'!

Not far away a Pawnee Chief
Broke a feathered lance.
On hearing of his fallen brave
He told his men to dance.

The Indians put on their paint
And swore the whites would pay,
And no one saw the Chief's young son
Run in the woods that day.
When Small Bear came on Tommy
His young heart felt no fear.
The youngsters stared as boys will do
Then grinned from ear to ear.
Together they climbed up a tree
And waded in the stream.
And when at last the moon came up
The boys lay down to dream.

When Tom's pa found him missin'
He went and got his gun.
The great Chief left the council fire,
Each man must find his son.

War party's comin'!
War party's comin'!

Into the woods the fathers ran,
They searched in every place,
Until above the sleeping boys
The men came face to face.

The red man picked up little Tom
And raised his scalping knife.
And Tommy's father drew his Colt
And threatened Small Bear's life.
They stood there in a silence
That seemed to have no end,
Till Small Bear asked his father,
Please, to spare his little friend.
The great Chief looked at his young son
Then gave Tom his release.
And Tommy's pa held out his hand
And said, "Let's talk of peace."
When word got to the wagons,
All heard the news with joy.
There'd be no bloody Indian raid.
Because of two small boys.

The lion,
So the Bible says,
Shall lay down with the lamb.
Today I saw a little child
Lead the way for man.

# WATER HOLE
*(Grades 4, 5 and 6.)*

I lost my dad and mother
When I was just a lad.
Uncle Pete was all
The family that I had.
One day Pete bought a wagon.
Said: "Boy, we're moving West,
I hear that California
Is the land that heaven blessed."

We rolled our prairie schooner
Out on the Western plain.
Drove smack into trouble
That Spring there'd been no rain.
The prairie was a furnace
Beneath the sun's hot glare.
You had to choke and struggle
Just to draw a breath of air.

Runnin' low on water
Pete was worried, I could see.
He'd hardly touch the dipper
So there'd be enough for me.
Water hole! Water hole!
How much farther must we roll
Before we get this wagon
To a water hole?

A stranger with a rifle
Appeared in front of us.
His tongue was dry and swollen,
His lips were caked with dust.
He screamed, "I'll take your water,
The sun has burned me dry,
And don't you try to stop me,
Not unless you want to die!"

He reached the water barrel
But Uncle Pete was fast.

His hand flew to his pistol,
I heard an awful blast.
The mad man staggered backward
Shot dead and fallin' down.
He crashed against the barrel
And it spilled out on the ground.

Uncle Pete was silent
As we drove on through that day,
And then he started ravin'
In a crazy sort of way.
"Water hole! Water hole!
Satan, I'd sell my soul
For just one drink of water
At a water hole."

Like magic we found water
Just over the next hill.
And Pete cried, "Thank you, Satan!"
Then ran and drank his fill.
But in that muddy water
Lay the bones of things long dead.
A buzzard dipped and circled
In the red sky overhead.

"I bargained with the devil,
And lost," said Uncle Pete,
"But though that drink was poison,
It tasted mighty sweet."
He died there on that desert
And I covered him with stones
To keep the turkey buzzards
From pickin' at his bones.

Oh Lord up there in heaven,
When it's time for judgin' Pete,
He bargained with the devil,

But was crazy with the heat.
Water hole! Water hole!
How much longer must I roll
Before I get this wagon
To a water hole?

It seemed my brain was boiling,
I knew that I'd soon drop.
When the mule team started runnin',
I couldn't make 'em stop.
And then I saw the reason,
And what a wondrous thing.
I saw a stand of willows
That circled 'round a spring.

Out west in California,
I guess I've done right well.
But I have not forgotten
That dusty burning hell,
Where men can go plum crazy,
And men will sell their souls
For just one drink of water
At a water hole.

Water hole!
Water hole!
For just one drink of water
At a water hole.

# PALOMINO
*(Middle School.)*

While ridin' the ridgeline above the Big Sur
In the barranca I saw somethin' stir.
A wild golden stallion with a mane white as snow
And I swore I'd corral me that palomino.

I tried hard to catch him for forty-nine days,
But I was outwitted in forty-nine ways.
Then up an arroyo I gets him boxed in.
And when I'd lassoed him the fight did begin.

    Palomino, palomino,
    I swore I'd corral me that palomino.

The strain on my saddle, it made the cinch bust,
That crazy hoss drags me a mile through the dust.
Then he pulls up real sudden and wheelin' around,
He comes back to stomp me right into the ground.

Well I took off a runnin' and went up a tree.
He circles below like he's laughin' at me.
But the rope I'd put on him was trailin' behind,
And in one of the branches it soon was entwined.

    Palomino, palomino,
    I swore I'd corral me that palomino.

He fought like a demon but the rope, it held fast.
And I said, "Palomino, I got you at last!"
He bucked for an hour, then he fell on his side,
And I knew he was mine when the hobbles were tied.

I set down plum tuckered and rolled me a smoke.
Studied the brave hoss that I had just broke,
He knew he was beaten, he'd lost all his fight,
And deep down inside me this didn't seem right.

    Palomino, palomino,
    I swore I'd corral me that palomino.

And then in an instant I knew what to do.

I pulled off the hobbles and cut the lasso.
He stood there a moment, just lookin' at me,
Like he's tryin' to thank me for settin' him free.

One slap on his flank and away he did fly.
And watchin' him vanish I starts in to cry.
Wherever I wander, wherever I go,
My heart is still back with that palomino.

Palomino, palomino,
My heart is still back with that palomino.

# MEDICINE HAT
*(Middle School.)*

You're in the town of Medicine Hat,
It's the year of the drought.
Out on the bone-dry prairie
Death walked all about.
The sun boiled up the river
Your cattle die of thirst.
The crops are burned and withered,
Things can't get much worse.

Then to the town of Medicine Hat
Came a rain-makin' man.
Said for a thousand dollars
He would save the land,
He'd bring the rain a splashin'
Like magic from the sky.
So you scrape to raise the cash
And you pay the man to try.
   And make rain,
   Gentle rain,
   Blessed rain.

The rainmaker gets a drum
And he commence to pound.
He sets a pot to boilin'
Till the steam churns all around.
Fills a sack with horntoads,
Paints a line across the ground,
But not a sign of rain
As the sun went down.

Outside the town of Medicine Hat,
Just before it was dawn,
You catch him with your money
He was movin' on.
You need no judge and jury,
He's guilty as can be,
So you string him up in fury

Out at the hangin' tree.

A man was hung in Medicine Hat,
And as the rope stretched tight,
A soft wind started blowin'
Rain clouds into sight.
You'd hung a cheat and faker,
Yet you are filled with shame
As you bury the rainmaker
And walk home in the rain.
   In the rain,
   Gentle rain,
   Blessed rain.

# CHRISTOPHER SUNSHINE
(Middle School.)


Once a young hitch-hiker
Stepped inside my car.
Said, "I am Christopher Sunshine
And I have traveled far."
And I've got things to tell you
Gifts that I will give.
I am Christopher Sunshine
And I've learned how to live.

He said:
    Everybody's got his own bag, Babe.
    You've got yours and I got mine.
    Everybody's got his own bag, Babe,
    And ain't that fine.

His hair was down to his shoulders,
His manner soft and shy.
It was Christopher Sunshine
Who looked me in the eye.
As we flew along the highway
The spinning wheels they turned,
And Mister Christopher Sunshine
Told me what he'd learned.

    *Chorus*

And I felt a feelin' of freedom
Lift this old heart of mine.
When he got out at the crossroads
He left a rose behind.
And that's what Christopher Sunshine
Gave me as a gift.
And then he put his thumb out
And caught another lift.

# TEENAGE CREATURE
*(Middle School.)*

I was a teenage creature
Tonight there's a werewolf moon
Come and hold my hairy hand
Down at the black lagoon.

I was a high school monster
A teenage Frankenstein.
Let me take you in my arms
And crush you one more time.

Gotta face like a dog
Feet like a frog
I'm covered with a lizard's scale
Gotta cut a hole in my ol' blue jeans
For my slimy tail.

I was a body snatcher
And you're the sweet earthling,
Do you think that you would dare
Go steady with the thing?

I was a teenage vampire
A rock and rollin' ghoul.
Won't you let a Dracula
Walk you home from school?

I live in a hole
Look like the mole
A horrible sight to see.
If you hear a growl I'm on the prowl
And baby you're for me.

I was a teenage spider
And you're my junior miss,
So give a boy tarantula
His very first kiss.

I was a teenage creature
I'm always scaring you,
So point a stake straight at my heart
And darling drive it through.

# WORDS ARE WEIRD AND HUMANS...?
*(High School.)*

Sometimes the English language
Will abandon you completely.
Like, have you ever gone looking for the word
You would use to describe
What it was you had left if you happened to lose
One of your galoshes?
What is that other rubber thing?
And goulash is Hungarian stew.

And I've got a "new" for you,
"New" being the singular of "news,"
Which is that words are weird,
And the weirdest words of all are the obscenities.
Like who invented these?
Where did they come from?

Did the English-speaking part of the world
Once hold a great convention?
The chair calling the restless throng to order,
Explaining that some ding dong
Would soon invent the automobile,
A thing
That would forever be breaking down,
Running out of gas and catching our fingers
In slamming doors,
                    Aghhhhh!

And for sanity's sake at least,
We should set aside some forbidden words to use
At times such as these,
To help let the steam out.
And rising to the occasion
A man of vision shouts from the back of the hall
"Mr. Chairperson!"
    (I'm for degenderization, but what do we do
    With words like "manhole?") "I suggest
That in the English-speaking part of the world

We use bodily functions as our obscenities."
The motion was seconded.
Carried unanimously.
The jubilant congregation staging
A wild twenty-minute demonstration,
Before settling down to the difficult task
Of hammering out the details,
Taking the most intimate human bodily function
And making it the most obscene.
Then completing the list,
Heavy on body parts and toilet procedure.

Clearly
It was one of humankind's finest hours,
And it simply had to be this way,
Because in other cultures,
What we consider obscene and insulting,
Means no more to them than like calling
A person a "big eye!"
A "little ear!"
A "son of a forehead!"

In the Orient, however,
Try calling a person a "pig"
Or a "dog" and see what happens.

I would guess at their great gathering
A dignified old gentleman rose to propose:
That here in the East
To call a human by an animal name
Should be the highest of insults.
And of course,
For this wisdom and insight, he was given
A standing but polite: Ahhh so!

And so it goes until every radio/TV talk show
Keeps a finger on the panic button: (beep beeping)
Out expletives
That have become so commonplace and innocuous,
Even sweet old ladies are overheard at teatime saying
Margaret, would you prefer one or two
(Beep beep) lumps?

49

And why?
Everyone knows what goes on behind the (beep beeps).
It must be that the media realizes
How overworked and useless these words have become,
And is now breaking ground for the day,
That when we stub our toe we can go hopping around
(beep beeping).

Perhaps now is the time
For another great obscenity assembly.
Time to outline this new dilemma
And once again throw the floor open for suggestions
So that
The ever-present man of brilliance
Can propose to thunderous applause:
"Mr. Chairperson, the old words have become impotent,
So I suggest we change and make the word
Nose
The filthiest dirtiest word in the English language."
After which, I suppose we would all
Step into the street going, "Nose Man, nose!"
"Kiss my nose!"
"Up your nose!"

There is a sad postscript to all of this,
However, which is
That in the name of tolerance
And understanding the Free Speech Movement
Has become so successful
We may have lost more than we gained.
For I find
I am left with nothing to use profane enough,
Obscene enough,
To describe the stupid waste and tragic death
Of Lenny Bruce.

# IN MY OWN FUNNY WAY
*(High School.)*


I was given four white pigeons
Young birds put in my care
And I built them a loft
Where they might stay.
You can say it was a prison
But I meant it for a home
And I brought them feed and water
Every day.

> You see I loved them
> No matter what you say
> God knows I loved them
> In my own funny way.

And I promised them their freedom
Promised them the sky
But only when I knew
They wouldn't stray.
And I warned them of the hunter
Who hunted on the hill
And of the hawk who waited
For her prey.

> You see I loved them
> No matter what you say
> God knows I loved them
> In my own funny way.

And then there came the morning
I forgot to hook the gate.
In an instant they were out
And in a tree
And I worried myself crazy
Trying to coax them back
But they paid little mind to me.

And I thought about the hunter
And I thought about the hawk

And I saw that they
Were bound to fly away.
So I went and took my shotgun
Down from the wall
And the thunder of it sounded
In the day.

But I loved them
No matter what you say
God knows I loved them
In my own funny way.

*(Kent State)*

# WHO'S WAVIN'
*(High School.)*

I ain't wavin' babe, I'm drownin'.
Goin' down in a cold lonely sea.
I ain't wavin' babe, I'm drownin'.
So babe quite wavin' at me.

I ain't laughin' babe, I'm cryin'.
I'm cryin', oh why can't you see?
I ain't foolin' babe, I ain't foolin',
So babe quit foolin' with me.

This ain't singin' babe, it's screamin'.
I'm screamin' that I'm gonna drown.
And you're smilin' babe, and you're wavin',
Just like you don't hear a sound.

I ain't wavin' babe, I'm drownin'.
Goin' down right here in front of you.
And you're wavin' babe, you keep wavin'.
Hey babe, are you drownin' too?

Oh.

# LONELINESS
*(High School.)*

Standing by a highway
Waiting for a ride
A bitter wind is blowing
Keeps you cold inside.
A line of cars is passing
No one seems to care
You look down at your body
To be sure you are there.

Sitting in a hotel
Staring at the walls
With cracks across the ceiling
And silence in the halls,
You open up the window
And turn the TV on
Then you go down to the lobby
But everybody's gone.

And this is loneliness
The kind that I have known,
If you've had times like this
My friend
You're not alone.

So you leave the empty city
And go down to the shore
You're aching to discover
What you're looking for.
The beaches are deserted
In the morning time
A solitary figure
You walk the water line.

Come upon a tidepool
And stand there peering in
And when you touch the water

The circles do begin.
They lead to where a seabird
Lies crumpled on the sand
So you take a single pebble
And hold it in your hand.

And this is loneliness
Another kind I've known,
If you've had times like this
My friend
You're not alone.

You come back up the beaches
At the end of day
And see how all your footprints
Have been washed away.
No
Nothing is forever
We are born to die,
So may I say I love you
Before I say goodbye.

I must say I love you
And now I'll say goodbye.

# III.
# FACULTY

# THE DRAGONFLY

i wish i could remember
what i knew when i was five
i think i had the answer then
having just recently arrived

i recall
that i could change into a dragonfly
and when you know how to do this
you know everything

no wonder i cried
when they sent me off
on that first day of school

# KINDERGARTEN LOGIC

how many mornings have i struggled
on the forest floor
trying to pull my pants on
inside a sleeping bag

cursing and muttering
in the darkness of that collapsible hole
looking for all the world
like some stricken giant green bug
writhing on the ground in its death throes

this morning i awoke clearheaded
and decided to stand like a man
and do it the easy way
and i did
and was stepping into them
just as slick as you please

when i heard this voice whispering

    someone will see you!

and in the chilly early-morning air
of that crowded campground
i stood there
pants half-mast
and thought about that
and it came to me in a blinding flash
the reason
we don't offer a course in logic
to kindergarten kids

# A PERFECT RED STRIPE

years ago it was there
your beauty
on something as simple as a square of paper

remember kindergarten?
and the yellow spot — the sun
    the splash of blue — the sky
    the curving
    dripping green line of the hills
and the perfect red stripe

remember how you looked at your work
and saw that it was good?

    what is this?
    teacher said
    questioning the red

    a fire engine

and then you looked at your work again
and then you hurled your brush
into the corner of the room
and stomped off defeated

later
out on the playground
you hit Barbara Jenkins in the head
with a kickball
and now you sit in the barber chair
hating yourself and the length of my hair
waiting for some kind of good fairy
to come down and save your ass

    but i remember
    i wish you did

## THE POET GOES INTO
## THE ELEMENTARY SCHOOL

good Lord!
it just came to me—
my shoes are older than almost
everyone
in this building

# SPIDERS!

when i was a little kid
another little kid told me
that if i poured water down a tarantula hole
i could get him to come out
so i did
        and he did
and bit me

since then spiders
have not been among my favorite things

last year i had occasion
to spend some time with an entomologist
that's a bug freak
and this nut was really into spiders
        beautiful creatures
that walk smoothly
four feet on the floor
not jerky like people
this dude didn't live in a house
he lived in a big jar full of 'em

and i got to thinking
that if someone ran up to us in the street
yelling
        spiders!
we'd 'a both known
what he was hollering about
but we would 'a knocked each other down
running in different directions

        when it comes to words
        it's a miracle we communicate at all

# INVENTING THE WHEEL

i don't often read other poets
and i'll tell you why

when i finally get around
to sitting down in the middle of the road
to invent the wheel
having spent days
gathering my materials around me
and having just figured out where to drill
the first hole
it's enough to make you break down and cry
to look up and see
some brilliant young S.O.B.
on a bicycle
              go pedaling by

# THE WAY TO TEACH

*(It isn't so much having a question*
*to ask, rather the ability to create one)*

and so
he let them have their games
until the tide was fully out
        and when it was
he came upon the rocky beach
a may-pole of a man
among the shouting children
and bending down beside a magic pool
        peering in
he waited

he waited till a ring of faces gathered
at the edge of this attention
then slowly reaching through the mirror
gave a sea anemone
        a punch
who did what sea anemones will do
quickly folding in
on what should have been a lunch

        WOW!

he said — eyes popping
then abruptly rising
but keeping in mind the length of his legs
moved on up the beach
        the children scrambling behind
        with questions

# BACK TO BASICS

from a system of education
wherein if it can't be measured
it will have to be ignored
comes word
        that an entire
        high school assembly
        required to sit through
        a poetry reading
        left at the bell
        convinced
        that they had just had
        a free period

the report
cannot be verified though
as the teaching staff
also took the event
to be a free period
and spent it in limbo
        otherwise known
        as the faculty room

and who can blame them?
they know you only emerge
from something like a spelling bee
with a clear unmistakable winner

the rest of us
the functionally illiterate 5,000
are left
with seven loaves and two fish
to divvy up for dinner

        and don't ask for more
        the age of miracles
        is past

# A BELL CURVE

if your carpenter
didn't know what batterboards were
you are probably living in a lopsided house
the carpenter's apprentice
will carry and stack a lot of lumber
learning his trade

and when it comes to brain surgeons
i believe in grades
bell curves and all that
i want to see him flunked out
long before he gets into my head
asking a nurse
what all the funny looking wrinkled stuff is
and God help the electrical engineer
who gets his wires crossed

but how do you grade a poem?

i mean wouldn't it be a little bit
like trying to grade a dream

     ah — student
     your dream started off well enough
     but fell all apart in the middle
     too much sex for sex sake
     and the ending was quite frankly trite
     at best this is a C- dream

parents — students — faculty — friends
what we have here is the finest trade school
in the history of the world
     period
so let's hear it for today's tool and die makers
and leave the dreamers be

# FOR THE ENTRANTS
# OF THE MISSISSIPPI JR. COLLEGE
# CREATIVE WRITING CONTEST

it being the South
the expectation was
that some unborn Capote
would leap from the competition
and take me by the throat
or
that i would find myself
forgiving
an adolescent Kathrine Ann Porter
for being a bit sophomoric
my picky criticism
punctured
by at least one poignant phrase

the reluctant judge
amazed in the end
and delivered
by a painfully green
yet promising James Dickey

alas
this was not to be
for either
i have gone blind
(always a possibility)
or
the needle in the haystack
simply wasn't there to find

in any case
i can only wonder now
would it have been easier
to pick an ace
from a pack of aces?

tomorrow
some latent William Faulkner
may emerge from all of this
and prove me wrong
but not sorry
a critic is never sorry
for
if you let my red pen
turn you from your love of language
to a desolate and dreary life
pumping gas
　　　　　　that then
　　　　　　is where you belong

# TERMINAL COOL

in the final stages of this cruel affliction
the diseased are often the last to know
how disfigured their demeanor has become

with me
it was not until friends began talking through the door
and wore flu masks
not until i began receiving mail addressed to Rex Reed
promotional material — color brochures pouring in
from leper colonies
not until then
did i bother to consult a mirror and see the result
of an unchecked case of skepticism

    the face
    once eager and receptive
    had lost all expression
    every trace of wonder and delight
    had sloughed off
    constant analysis had narrowed the eyes
    paralysis had folded the arms
    and there
    at the corner of my mouth — a hand
    horribly grafted in place

the ghastly sight shot me with a chill
there was no doubt about it
i was critically ill

infected i suspect
by an English professor i once knew
or by ingesting too many clever book
and movie reviews
but the question is academic
you simply don't care when you are the lump
slumping down in the chair

recently however —
at fifty
i have experienced the miracle of remission

at a sophisticated New York cocktail party
suddenly and for no reason
the feeling came flooding back
and i heard myself blurting out
publicly
       that i secretly enjoyed *The Sound of Music*
       and watch *Little House on the Prairie*

       that i have been moved to tears
       by a McDonalds ad

       even
       that i can think of at least one
       poem by Rod McKuen
       that's not bad

the next time Peter Pan throws pixie dust
asking the audience to stand
and applaud Tinker Bell back to life
the next time
if my luck holds
i'll be able to do it

# THE TEACHER ALONE

i suppose anyone fat-headed enough
to stand up in front of more
than one person and try to say something
                    deserves what he gets

but if you're being rude
because you've spent so much time
with your television set

ignoring Walter Cronkite
and/or
beating your toy on the floor
in front of Captain Kangaroo
that you've gone and lost sight
of reality
then i must respond
and call you on it

if i don't
and just let it slide
i might as well be on TV
and this room really is twenty-four inches
wide
and absolutely empty

# THE COUNSELOR

i was talking to myself again
in front of the mirror
but the glass man only
moved his lips with mine
and said nothing that would help

so i came to you to hear
what it was i had to tell myself
i chose you above everyone else
because i knew
that you would say

     one can
     only
     help oneself

and that is exactly
the kind of smart-ass remark
i will not take
off a mirror

# WHALES—OFF PALO COLORADO

today i saw the whales
moving south along the coast
and had to stop the car and get out
and stand there just watching

one of them came in close to shore
and i thought to myself then
that the whole journey would be worth it
just to see the magic of this Atlantis — rising
blowing and steaming from the sea — an island
of life
      today i saw the whales and i was healed

i can tell you now of the dancers — the three girls
and the dark wet highway — and the car
that came hurtling into their young lives
and how the rain fell for five days as we followed
slowly behind black limousines — three times
slowly with our lights on

but the sun returned this morning
and the rain has washed the air clean
and brought the Ventana mountains in so close
they cut my eyes
      sometimes it hurts to see things clearly

for those girls the dance had just begun
but they went out dancing
trailing veils behind them and somehow
this simple act tells me that they too paused
somewhere along the way and saw
      the whales moving south along the coast
      on a day like today
i hope you will forgive me
for trying to put order and sense to it all
but if i don't can you tell me who in hell will?

# THE SECOND HALF

i turned forty a while ago
and came dribbling out of the locker room
ready to start the second half
glancing up at the scoreboard
i saw that we were behind
    7 to 84
and it came to me then
    we ain't gonna win
and considering the score
i'm beginning to be damn glad
this particular game ain't gonna go on
    forever

but don't take this to mean i'm ready
for the showers
take it to mean i'm probably gonna play
one helluva second half

i told this to some kids in the court
next to mine and they laughed
but i don't think they understood
    how could they
playing in the first quarter only one point
    behind

deep into autumn
the third period
i have discovered
that winning the game
is not what is important

what is important though
is
that i look good
while losing

# BURNOUT (A MISNOMER)

burnout
you've seen the results
in the shop on the shelf
row after row of grey empty faces
with nothing happening in the glassy eyes
except
a little surface reflection

burnout
you know the symptoms. . .
a history of dependable service
then suddenly for no reason things go dark
and you're a dead piece of furniture
waiting
to be removed from the living room

burnout
the psychological repairman said
and shrugged and shook his head
having checked everything
except the cord
which of course
                    was disconnected
in a word unplugged

and to think
i nearly went to the dump myself
because someone less than a poet
trying to describe a condition
came up with a misleading term
clearly
a case of burnout demands a second opinion
and this is mine
                  find an outlet
                  and if the cord doesn't reach
                  move the set

# REQUIEM
*For Sharon Christa McAuliffe*


some say that you
and the Challenger crew
came to a tragic end
but when i recount the story
of your star-crossed flight
when i describe the circumstance
surrounding your death
i will do so in the same breath
i use to tell about a comic
who died
at the height of his career
on stage cracking a joke
—the audience roaring

and so dear teacher
the tears are not for you
but for an assembly
of cheering students
there to wish you bon voyage
it was Times Square New Year's Eve
until the explosive arrival
of childhood's end
the premature loss of innocence
caught
wearing a birthday party hat
clutching a tin kazu
no dear teacher
the tears are not for you

the grief i feel
is for the other finalists
the nine who missed the boat
one minute wrestling with envy
the next flooded with relief
countervailing emotions separated only
by a startling puff of smoke

the castaways drenched with guilt
at what they felt
when the call came
and they were granted
a last-minute reprieve
i grieve for them dear teacher
not for you

but most of all i'm angry
at myself for being fascinated
by the telescopic view
of your forlorn family
huddled on the dock
waving goodbye to the Titanic
and angrier still that i would sit
watching grainy pictures
shot from ambush
of small children
getting in and out of limousines
for this rude intrusion
i am truly sorry
but not for you

dear teacher
how can i be anything
but overjoyed
for someone
destined to spend eternity
aboard a great plumed ship
steaming out
across a bay of cobalt blue
you
at the rail
dreaming
forever leaning toward Orion

# IV.
# & FRIENDS

## The Primary School—
# CHECKING OUT THE MERCHANDISE

The sky was blue and cloudless. The desert was warm and dusty. The drive to Casa Grande was more than an hour southeast of Phoenix. I wanted to meet Ric Masten in another setting before my school shared his day a week later. What could a middle-aged man bring to the lives of six-year-olds? I pulled into the small city library and found it bolted shut. A van of noisy children marched into a side door. I followed them and found a pre-school class and was given a printed notice that I had the poet day and place all wrong! He had spoken there yesterday and was perhaps somewhere at the high school today.

A high school office is the amazing site of truancy excuses, scheduling confusion and telephone requests. The students waiting for discipline decisions slumped along the bench. "Is Ric Masten speaking here today?" No one knew. The clerk was on break. Pupils and administrators streamed in and out. I didn't seem noticed or linked by profession to any of them. The schooling process was grinding on. Learning and growing must be going on somewhere else.

I was eventually directed to the auditorium. All the huge doors were locked but one. I entered onto the stage area where a small bearded man was reciting a poem with passion and power. I passed a smiling teacher standing against the side wall. I walked around a grim supervisor with a clipboard. I found a seat in the back row with the boys.

I was neither the unfriendly office workers, or the hard-eyed slumping students or the unsmiling supervisor. I was the one captivated by the growing warmth of eyes, the opened hearts, the rapt attention and the strong voice coming from behind the podium. I stayed to the end and watched the audience worked by an expert. I heard stories of personal learning disabilities, examples of terrific and horrible poetry and warnings to tell someone at home they were loved before it was too late. Sure, some struggling teens balked at the harshness of the reminders at them, but softened hearts and introspection were evident.

Having finally found my way to this school poet, I joined him and his wife for a quick coffee stop and then off to the hardest of all his performances — a county nursing home. Ric told me this would be a sample of his kindergarten program. I watched the hugs Billie Barbara entered with, the moist eyes of the residents, the toe tapping and the weakly clapping hands. I sat on the floor with the wheelchairs to join in the event. I could see the value of going from one spoken poem to another, from guitar to voice, from Billie's honesty of personal struggles, to the room briefly coming to renewed life with joy, hope and faint courage.

I could also see how exhausting the travel circuit really is—with schools, libraries and rest homes for these two poetic sojourners. From here they were to appear on radio broadcasts and perform at a church and college in Phoenix. We parted from their heavily laden van to meet again on a rainy Monday to spend a day at my primary school with young people who are demanding, draining, curious and full of gifts and spunk.

It's a half year later now and some children still ask me about Ric. Some teachers were moved enough to read and teach some poetry and sent these first efforts to the Mastens. Our creative writing and poetry workshops continue in a slightly different form now. The business of trying and failing and learning to find oneself again continues in various ways. But for a brief day, we laughed and smiled and sang and celebrated together the love of words and the meaning of being friends by sharing something much deeper, nobler and fun.

Sherrie Dewey Moritz
*Primary Gifted Coordinator*
*Osborn School District*
*Phoenix, Arizona*

**The Junior High —**

# "BUT HE SAID HE'S DONE PRISONS"

I was more than a little embarrassed to so suddenly be sharing with students the intimate details that were appearing on the seventh grade science class movie screen. A model of a male member was being shown in various stages of erection. I, a mere English teacher, was hoping that the science teacher for whom I was covering would be back before the film was over, in case there were, God forbid, questions. However, I was also impressed with our school system for providing such frank and complete information on this subject of such survival importance.

A small blond girl started towards me in the darkened room. I panicked. What did she want? "Ms. Harris, I'm going to be sick"? "Ms. Harris, my mother doesn't want me to watch this"? How would I handle it?

In a whisper she addressed me. "Ms. Harris, when's lunch?"

Junior high students. Essence of non sequitur. A California education official told me recently that in our state these students are configured in 27 different ways—grades 6, 7, 8, or 7,8, or 7, 8, 9 or 24 other possible combinations.

That bespeaks the chaos that surrounds them—girls still carrying dolls sit in my class next to painted women not yet in control of their medium. I call on a boy to answer a question, then I and the whole class agonize with him as his changing voice betrays him with alternating squeaks and growls.

What do these kids want with a rumpled nonconformist poet carrying an old-fashioned guitar with no amp? As he enters the classroom, anyone can see he's not from their planet; even their parents and teachers are more in style. They look around, embarrassed, to align their response to their classmates'. And I, who have brought these two disparate forces together, wonder whatever possessed me. Ric's feelings will surely be hurt, and I'll be phoning some homes tonight to harangue about rudeness to our class guest.

83

But he said he's done prisons, I remind myself. They must be as bad.

He begins, and, while initially they don't seem to know exactly how to respond, at least they're generally quiet. I'm the only one to laugh at the first few funny things he says, and the whole class turns around to look at me. But he is a showman, and by the time he straps his guitar on and renders, "The Dirty Word Song," he's got them. "Doggie pooh!" he exults, and they thrill to the forbidden, to sharing the joke. On occasion they even forget to check their neighbor's response, so caught up are they in the flow of his words.

But he's not here to entertain, and he doesn't take the easy way out by keeping them laughing. He tells them that his first poem got an F. He tells them about the time he considered suicide, and how writing about it helped.

And they're really staying with him!! "This is loneliness," he sings, "the kind that I have known." I sneak looks at my dear funny students, and see such naked loneliness in some of their faces that I have to look away.

He draws on the chalkboard a crude fence, and tells them that his craft is "putting a line of language around a feeling." He's doing a hard sell on the value of learning to say what you mean. The very real survival value of knowing how to use words. A veritable Language Arts commercial!

Heady stuff for an English teacher like myself, who, when asked at cocktail parties what I do, get told, "Oh, English. You know, I cannot for the life of me find a secretary who can spell."

He takes us all the way. In 45 minutes the class has gone from scoffers to celebrants. Past pain to prevailing. He sings, "I the caterpillar . . . so fragile and so frail," and tears stream down my face, and a few students see and poke others who in turn look. That's okay, though; we are bound together in a shared experience, and no longer is anything at anyone else's expense.

These pupae of mine—these awkward, scared, over-whelmed kids—have gotten to be, along with me, for a few moments, "tangled in the strings" of a real poet.

84

Education is a thrilling business. We educators are the eternal optimists; lately we have come to believe we can even cut down on child abuse by educating the potential abusees. We teach about sex, yes, and athletics and typing and how to be informed citizens. But Ric—standing in for all the world's writers—came to our school and showed us how words weave it all together. He showed us how to notice and record and share—how to make order from chaos—how many of life's vagaries can be tamed and shaped with just a pencil.

Helen Harris
*English Teacher*
*Chipman Middle School*
*Alameda*, California

## The High School—
# HOW MUCH DO I OWE YOU?

How many years has it been? I think it has been thirteen or fourteen years of important and very meaningful association. This poet came into my life and into the school's fabric back in those "revolutionary years." He was real hip—a chip off the old radical block with the appropriate language and dress to make any of our rebellious youth feel like they had met their savior. Frankly, Ric irritated the hell out of me on that first meeting. Playing to the crowd did not have to mean looking and talking like them. Anyway, he stayed for three days—that was the contract. At one point while addressing the school assembly, he had the audacity to say that the reason he was so damn good was because he had THE POWER. I couldn't believe he said that and told him so as quickly as I could get to him. You might believe you have THE POWER but you don't tell that to a vulnerable teenage group. All this was a most unusual beginning for such a lasting friendship, and despite my initial reaction, when he left our school on that very first of many visits, I felt as if my best friend had left town.

Educationally, we have had a very good working relationship. Our students had contact with Ric from those short three-day visits when the wizard did his magic to an expanded ten-day stay at Ric and Billie Barbara's home in California: spend ten days in a poet's home, see the Big Sur area, corral your feelings with words, think like the poet—the kids loved it. I loved it! We did the chores, worked the garden, cooked the meals, took trips up and down that beautiful coast experiencing and sharing and writing. Ric the wizard continued to do his magic, giving all the students and the faculty a very strong educational uplift. Of course, all the while I was trying to lure Ric and Billie back to Proctor. "Come with me, all your needs will be taken care of at our school." Finally, those words, a reasonable chunk of cash, and a desire to try it back East brought Ric and Billie to our campus. This time it was not for three days or ten days, but for a full nine-week term. The poet/magician was going to become a full-time teacher. Life would be different. Ric and Billie spent the spring term with us—please no snow! He was our first poet-in-residence. We had no plan other than to have Ric weave himself into the educational fabric of the school. Science, history, and English classes shared this poet/teacher's thoughts. He even taught an English elective and read once a week to our school assembly. It was an interesting relationship. Ric the poet/magician became the poet/teacher. No more quick, powerful strikes on the minds of the student body and then as quick an exit. Now he had to hang around and deal day in and day out with the power of his words and with those wonderfully frustrating, distracting, considerate, irresponsible, and loveable teenagers. The student body and faculty also had to make room for and adjust to the ever-present poet. The poet's words couldn't so easily be forgotten since his very presence in the hallways, classrooms, assembly, and dining hall brought his words instantly to mind. We all grew from the nine-week association. But what was the measurable result of the experience? Ric left us a book of our student poems to remember in a concrete way, his being among us and our student efforts. But it was also the immeasurable aspect of his being with us that will last. There were minds that were touched. The deepest, most sensitive part of each of us was stirred. It was that window to our soul that was flung open allowing us an opportunity to find new ways to express ourselves.

God bless the poet for he allows us to acknowledge the unbroken ribbon of our humanness.

David Fowler
*Headmaster*
*Proctor Academy*
*Andover, New Hampshire*

## The College—
# RIC MASTEN: ONE OF OUR FAILURES

Two years ago, Ric Masten was asked to give the keynote address at the annual Arizona English Teacher's Conference in Phoenix. It was a slice of life's irony so rich in lessons for us that I could not resist pointing to it when I introduced him that day. "Ladies and gentlemen," I said to the gathered audience of about four hundred English teachers, "I would like to introduce Ric Masten, one of our failures. . . ."

Because it was true. Years before, when he was in our English classes in junior high and high school, we failed Ric: with our red pens in our hands and righteousness in our eyes, we told him that he could not write. And on that October afternoon in Phoenix, many years and hundreds of beautiful-meaningful poems later, we were paying him $400 to come back and talk to us for an hour about writing. I would hope that we can learn from that irony—and from the irony of this collection of poetry, written by one of our failures.

Ric Masten is one of our failures in several ways. First, he is one of our failures because we did fail him—we flunked him. We told him that he was dumb and that he could not write. We made him ashamed of his own words; we turned him away from the gift that was in him. Basically, we told him that he could not write because—in his case—he could not spell. And in our smallness, we have often equated spelling (and grammar and punctuation) with the *real* act of language, which is deep and complex and powerful far beyond these small acts of editing. And so we flunked Ric Masten—and millions of others like him before and since.

But Ric was not dumb (nor have the other millions been). In Ric's case, he suffered (largely because we chose to make him suffer) from dyslexia—"neurological impairment of the ability to read." But listen to what Marilyn Ferguson tells us (in *The Aquarian Conspiracy*) about dyslexia:

> Dyslexia, which afflicts at least 10 percent of the population, seems to be associated with a dominance by the right cerebral hemisphere in

88

the reading process. Those with strong holistic perception are often handicapped by our educational system with its emphasis on symbolic language and symbolic mathematics. They have initial difficulty in processing these symbols. Yet this neurological minority may also be unusually gifted. They typically excel in the arts and in innovative thinking. Ironically, their potential contribution to society is frequently diminished because the system undermines their self-esteem in their first school years. (p. 299)

As the blind high priests of language, we could not see this. We could only see misspelled words. And so, we took (or tried to take) the gift of language away from Ric Masten.

Ric, then, is one of our failures in another way: *we* failed him. We failed to help him—because of our own blindness—to see and nurture and develop the gift of language that was in him even then. We did not have to see or believe that he would become a published poet—few of our students will do that. But we did need to see and believe that the gift of language—as a tool for psychological and spiritual survival—was in him then. Because it was. As it is in all of us, whether or not we can spell.

I wrote a poem myself once, a poem about the grimness of this left-brained blindness in our education, a poem about a small boy on his way to school one morning. . .

Along the road to the gray stone school,
he found a ragged butterfly
blazing out its life beside a pool
of last night's autumn rain
(the wind had brought a crimson leaf to lie
beside the yellow butterfly);
all this was wrapped with music in his mind—
but then from the gray stone school
the indifferent bell summoned him to find
death of quite another kind.

And so it has been all too often in our schools. And so it was with Ric. But in his case, there is good news in spite of all this—because he is one of our failures in yet another way. Ric is also one of our failures because he failed to believe us when we told him he was dumb and because he failed to let us take his language away from him. You see, Ric was just mean and stubborn enough that he wouldn't quite buy what we told him back then. Granted, it took him a while, but eventually he found out what real language was all about. And when he did, his "giftedness" began to emerge; and he began to write poetry that touched people and that spoke to them beneath the surface of their lives.

The turning point came when Ric made that same discovery about language that Eldridge Cleaver made while he was in Folsom Prison— that writing is so much more than a matter of spelling and punctuation. Cleaver says it in those few powerful words from *Soul On Ice:* "That is why I started to write. To save myself." And William Stafford, another poet, speaks of that same crucial insight about language when he has the muse in one of his poems speak these words: "When/you allow me to live with you, every/glance at the world around you will be/a sort of salvation."

In spite of the lack of help from us, Ric Masten eventually found his muse. He discovered by himself what his language was for—and he set about using it to save himself. That is what this collection is all about. That is, as Ric himself will tell you, what his poetry is all about. And saving oneself has little to do with spelling and commas and semicolons; rather, it has to do with saying one's feelings. Or, in Ric's own words, "putting a corral of words around the stuff that's in our gut and our heart."

So, I am glad that Ric is one of our failures in this third sense. I am glad that he now goes about the country undoing for others what was done to him. I am glad that he gives his gift so freely. He teaches us well. And in our gray stone schools, I hope that we who profess to teach writing are at last beginning to learn the lesson of this poet who is one of our failures.

G. Lynn Nelson
*Arizona State University*
*Tempe, Arizona*

## BOOKS

Also available on order, through local bookstores that use R. R. Bowker Company BOOKS IN PRINT catalogue system

☐ NOTICE ME! by Ric Masten        **Paperback $6.00**
For Parents, Students, Faculty & Friends
110 pages. ISBN 0-931104-17--3

☐ THEY ARE ALL GONE NOW
. . . And So Are YOU by Ric Masten     **Paperback $6.00**
106 pages. ISBN 0-931104-15-7

☐ EVEN AS WE SPEAK by Ric Masten.     **Paperback $5.50**
112 pages. ISBN 0-931104-12-2

☐ the DESERTED ROOSTER by Ric Masten.     **Paperback $5.00**
96 pages. ISBN 0-931104-11-4

☐ STARK NAKED by Ric Masten.     ☐ **Paperback $5.00**
110 pages. ISBN 0-931104-04-1     ☐ **Hardcover $10.00**

☐ VOICE OF THE HIVE by Ric Masten.     **Paperback $5.00**
104 pages. ISBN 0-931104-02-5

☐ DRAGONFLIES, CODFISH & FROGS by Ric Masten.     **Paperback $5.50**
112 pages. ISBN 0-931104-06-8

☐ HIS & HERS by Ric & Billie Masten.     **Paperback $5.00**
80 pages. ISBN 0-931104-01-7

☐ BILLIE BEETHOVEN     **Paperback $5.00**
by Billie Barbara Masten.
96 pages. ISBN 0-931104-13-0

## TAPES

☐ Ric Masten Singing
LET IT BE A DANCE     **Price $5.95**
12 Songs. Stereo SF-1002

## BROADSIDES . . . **Price $1.00**

Single sheets printed on colored stock. 8½"x11", suitable for framing.

☐ The Warty Frog        ☐ Let It Be a Dance
☐ The Second Half       ☐ The Homesick Snail
☐ Water Spots

## PUBLICITY PAMPHLETS

☐ Ric Masten in Concert . . . ☐ On the College Campus.
☐ In the High School . . . ☐ In the Middle School.
☐ In the Elementary . . . ☐ In the Church . . . ☐ On Relationships.
☐ Honorarium and Fee Schedule.

. . . . . . . . . . . . . . . . . . . . . . . . . . . . . . . . . . . . . . . . . . . . . . . . . . . . . . . .

CHECKS MADE OUT TO

## SUNFLOWER INK
Palo Colorado Canyon
Carmel, CA 93923

ORDER $ _____

6% SALES TAX (CA. RES.) _____

SHIPPING & HANDLING $ ___$1.25___

TOTAL $ _____

Name _____

Address _____

City _____ State _____ Zip _____